Pointing Home

Pointing Home

Poems by

Catherine Chandler

© 2019 Catherine Chandler. All rights reserved. This material may not be reproduced in any form, published, reprinted, recorded, performed, broadcast, without the express written consent of Catherine Chandler. All such actions are strictly prohibited by law.

Cover design by Shay Culligan
Cover photograph by Deno Pantelakos

ISBN: 978-1-949229-77-6

Kelsay Books
502 S. 1040 E. A116
American Fork, Utah 83004
www.kelsaybooks.com

For my children, Caitlin and Steven,
and granddaughters, Moriah, Martika, Shaela and Melina,
with love

Dejaría en este libro
toda mi alma.

—Federico García Lorca, "Este es el prólogo"

Acknowledgments

First and foremost, I would like to express my gratitude to the editors of the following journals in which these poems first appeared or are forthcoming:

Able Muse: "La Niña" ("Drought"), "Shakespeare's Sisters," "For Tim, on the Eve of Battle"; *The Agonist:* "Edward Hopper's *Pennsylvania Coal Town* (1947)," "Matthew 7:1-5," North on 81"; *Alabama Literary Review:* "Ending," "Nines," "My Father's Shirts," "The Woodlot," "Lessons at Fall Kill Creek"; *Angle:* "Dawn" ("Daybreak on the Peninsula"*)*; *Antiphon:* "Pentimento: *High Noon* (1949)"; *First Things:* "Votive"; *Light:* "There are always more fish in the sea;" *Literary Bohemian:* "Watershed"; *The Lyric:* "Pointing Home," "Slow Burn"; *Measure:* "Celebration," "We," "The Watchers at Punta Ballena, Uruguay," "Family at Sunset Beach, California"; *Mezzo Cammin:* "shadow art streaming from sly stone angels," "Edward Hopper's *Early Sunday Morning* (1930)"; *North of Oxford:* "Far into the Lives of Other Folk"; *Off the Coast:* "Interim"; *The Orchards:* "Secret Swig"; *Presence:* "Traversing the Circle of Fifths"; *Quadrant:* "Scintillae"; *The Raintown Review:* Four poems from "Madison Street" ("One-way Street"); *The Rotary Dial:* "Plain Beauty," "Robbie Bennett" ("Summer of 1970"); *Think:* "Multiverse."

I also wish to thank the following poets and/or literary executors for permission to publish my English translations in this collection: Álvaro Díaz (for Amanda Berenguer), Nidia di Giorgio (for Marosa di Giorgio), Paula Einöder, Jorge Arbeleche (for Juana de Ibarbourou), Circe Maia, Cristina Peri Rossi, Ana Inés Larre Borges (for Idea Vilariño), and Ida Vitale. The works of María Eugenia Vaz Ferreira and Delmira Agustini are in the public domain.

Special thanks to Rhina P. Espaillat and Timothy Murphy, and to my family on two continents in two hemispheres.

Contents

I. North on 81

North on 81   19

II. Lessons at Fall Kill Creek

Lessons at Fall Kill Creek   23
There are always more fish in the sea   24
My Father's Shirts   25
The Woodlot   26
Interim   28
We   29
Matthew 7:1-5   30
On Reading the Report, August 14, 2018   31
Traversing the Circle of Fifths   32
Plain Beauty   33

III. Madison Street

Overture   37
Sputnik   38
Slow Burn   39
Skip   40
Thinking of Happiness, She Thinks of That   41
Robbie Bennett   42
Retail Therapy   43
Phil   44
Bully   45

Grouper	46
Nanny Brown	47
Realpolitik	48
Intermezzo	49
"Doc" Baumann	50
Cat Lady	51
Changing of the Guard	52
Strange Gods	53
Kidnapped	54
Mrs. Moffat	55
Ragman	56
Mea culpa	57
Boots	58
Fire	59
Kitty Kramer	60
Coda	61

IV. Other Folk

Far into the Lives of Other Folk	65
Roxham Road	66
Shakespeare's Sisters	67
i. Suzy	67
ii. "Poetisa"	68
iii. Cinéma Vérité	69
Multiverse	70
Hapax legomenon	71

Nines	72
Χάος	73
Family at Sunset Beach, California	74
shadow art streaming from sly stone angels	75
For Tim, on the Eve of Battle	78
Votive	79
Edward Hopper Triptych	80
Early Sunday Morning (1930)	80
Pentimento: *High Noon* (1949)	81
Pennsylvania Coal Town (1947)	82

V. The Watchers

The Watchers at Punta Ballena, Uruguay	85
Su casa es mi casa	86
Secret Swig	86
The Split	87
Daybreak	88
Midday	89
Housework	90
Residual	91
Poem X	92
Steps	93
Prayer	94
Broken Poem	95
La Niña	96
Dawn	97

Ending	98
Celebration	99
Scintillae	100
Watershed	101

VI. Pointing Home

Pointing Home	105
Notes	107

I.

North on 81

North on 81

His native home deep imag'd in his soul.
—Alexander Pope (1688-1744), *The Odyssey of Homer*

Once more I linger by the house. The door
needs paint, a section of the fence is down,
the mailbox hangs askew. How they would frown
on such disinterest and neglect . . .
                              Once more
I step along a grass and granite row,
assailed by bloodroot, the insistent drone
of bees, a smack of dust and ashes, and
the sheer immensity of the unknown.
Once more, I rendezvous in no man's land—
no answers. Intimations.
                              Even so,
I visit for awhile, as mourners do;
then as I head back, north on 81,
past Scranton, Susquehanna, Binghamton . . .
once more the Endless Mountains fade from view.

II.

Lessons at Fall Kill Creek

Lessons at Fall Kill Creek

> Altissima quaeque flumina minimo sono labi.
> —Quintus Curtius Rufus, *Historiae Alexandri Magni*

I was only five, but I've not forgotten.
You and I set off as we do each morning.
Hand in hand, we walk in the April sunshine,
      father and first-born.

Halfway to the Samuel Morse School, we would
sometimes stop to see how the creek was faring—
Fall Kill Creek that runs through Poughkeepsie, draining
      into the Hudson.

Rain from upstate wetlands and marshes—seeping,
racing southward, coursing through stonewall channels—
forms a perfect habitat for the bluegill,
      darter and minnow.

Now we're at the Catharine Street and Mansion
crossing, looking over the iron railing
at the water, higher than ever, flowing
      steady and silent.

Then your quiet words—how it is that stillness
mustn't be confused with a lack of passion;
why it is that rivulets lead to rivers,
      rivers to oceans.

There are always more fish in the sea

. . . is all her mother had to say,
served up stale as réchauffé.
And as she wept, her young heart breaking,
other girls went fishing, taking
flatfish, catfish, ratfish, gar,
pike, perch, pollock, Arctic char,
sturgeon (for the caviar).
Fifty years on, she's still aching
for the one that got away.

My Father's Shirts

I've dusted, vacuumed, mopped the kitchen floor,
hung out the wash, swatted every fly—
it's Saturday, and yet there's one more chore.

The eldest child of seven, it is I
who's been entrusted with his shirts. Last night
I sprinkle-dampened them, then rolled them tight.
Today, from collar, yoke, and cuffs, to sleeves,
to pocket, placket, front and back, the dry,
hot iron makes the cotton steam. Nearby,
my mother checks for creases. As she leaves,
a side-glance at the gussets and the pleat.

I bristle, being too young to know that she
just hopes and prays I'll learn to take the heat.
And maybe live a good life, wrinkle-free.

The Woodlot

Eleven years ago we bought this house,
a cottage on a quiet lane, where trees
dominate the landscape, where the Ville
de Saint-Lazare protects its woods and wetlands
with an environmental bylaw bible
thicker than the girth of any oak
or sugar maple sapling one may wish
to cut without a permit from a stern
and rigorous inspector. So it was
we moved into our house one mid-October
and filled over a hundred bags with leaves
we'd raked until our backs and hands could take
no more of it. There were about a dozen
trees in our backyard, but the lot behind
was brush and bramble underneath a stand
of ash and linden, ironwood and one—
just one—white birch. It was a wooded lot,
and it had been the clincher on the deal:
no rear neighbors. We'd have bought
it if we could. *Some day.* Or so we thought.

You and those trees, he groused, a mild reproach,
because he, too, enjoyed the privacy
and loved the flocks of chickadees who fed
from outstretched hands, the squirrels and rabbits who
built their dreys and warrens in that wood.
Wild raspberries were plentiful in summer;
each spring trillium and columbine
shot up to ease the slap of April snow;
and often frigid January seemed
less so, as northern cardinals' *wheet! wheet! wheet!*
whistled through the branches of the lot
that bordered on our dog's last resting place.

Last year in early May the land was sold,
and all the trees, including the lone birch,
were felled, chain-sawed and hauled away. The laws
I mentioned don't apply (so I've been told)
to new construction, and a house was built.
A matching shed. A five-foot chain-link fence
secures new neighbors from the likes of me—
the one who trespassed. She who hugged that tree.

Interim

They circle slow, slow, through the day
like two hands on a silent clock
that overlap at certain times
but only for a moment, then
go on their separate ways again.

She ponders Yeats *(Things fall apart . . .)*
yet smiles on cue at ten to ten,
as metaphors and perfect rhymes
—perhaps more artifice than art—
drip, drip, like honey from her pen.

They used to laugh, they used to talk,
they used to have so much to say;
now midnight conversations keep
to topics far, far, from the heart

and languish as the seconds sweep.

We

We grieve for the twelve trees we lost last night,
and for the upswept years they took to grow.
The shingles we thought strong and weather-tight
went flying through the roiling indigo.

The lower forty's flooded, and the power
lines are down. The welcome mat is gone.
The red light on a distant cell phone tower
blinks wearily above this dénouement.

As we lie weakened, silent, back to back,
our feeble weaponry a feint of sleep,
our dwelling place a darkened cul-de-sac,
we grieve for those twelve trees, but cannot weep.

The tumult of the west wind drawing near,
we weigh our options. Go for one more year.

Matthew 7:1-5

The fix. The stealth. The stoop. The swoop. The kill—
a barb more brutal than a falcon's bill.

Words meant to wound. *What are you on, some kind
of guilt trip?* (So much for the ties that bind).

The bushwhacked, speck-eyed brother turns away.
He'll keep his counsel till another day,

trusting their mother hasn't heard, although
her sense of hearing was the last to go.

—Hospice of the VNA, Heritage House

On Reading the Report, August 14, 2018

Our lives were stolen by a man in black,
and we will never ever get them back.

Traversing the Circle of Fifths

Backward I turn, past tones and semitones,
in search of consolation, consonance,
on pathways running, wrapping more than once
around the circle. As I play these tunes
on my piano as the solstice nears,
their facile resolutions contravene
my long search for a god from the machine,
the Star of Bethlehem, the angel choirs.

Far away, my daughter's daughter dreams
of sugarplums. So, tell me, who am I,
world-weary, to suggest as truth or lie,
that underneath the snow a white rose blooms;
or worse, as sad notes fall into each other,
that Santa is her father and her mother?

Plain Beauty

Glory be to God for homely things—
    For muddy boots and oil-stained dungarees;
        For calloused hands that knead and scrub and hem;

Threadbare baby blankets; apron strings;
    A copybook of blotted ABCs;
        And drowsy lullabies at 3 a.m.

All things modest, unassuming, rough;
    Rag rugs, first drafts, eucalyptus trees;
        Plain-spoken poems *(foliage . . . leaf and stem);*

They whelm the world in love. It's not enough.
        Love them.

III.
Madison Street

Madison Street

Overture

Imagine this: a narrow one-way street
in northeast Pennsylvania long ago,
between two Asian wars, a neighborhood—
a little world of sweet and bittersweet,
where children didn't know they didn't know,
and things were either bad or they were good.
We didn't get the gist of dirty jokes;
we actually believed the monkey hoax.
So, here's to us who didn't know the score,
who idolized Hank Aaron and Annette;
who pilfered Slo-Pokes from the corner store
or from an aunt, a Newport cigarette;
whose plain speech never lapsed to metaphor,
and party lines comprised our Internet.

Sputnik

October sundown, nineteen fifty-seven.
Frank De Luca stands outdoors because
of something curious orbiting above.
Just five, he still believes in saints and heaven,
the Easter Bunny, Batman, Santa Claus,
the Golden Rule, God's everlasting love.
His dad points to the Soviet satellite
whose certain, silent, drifting, line of flight
convinces them the moon and maybe Mars
could someday be a new frontier for man.
But Frank will soon discard all avatars
except for one. Bereaved, the boy will scan
the endless arc for signs of shooting stars,
and in his dreams soar! soar! like Peter Pan.

Slow Burn

The children miss their favorite swimming hole
up at the creek, now autumn's settled in.
This afternoon, one of Glen Alden's trucks
has brought a mix of pea and chestnut coal.
They'll chute it down into our cellar bin—
four tons, just over eighty-seven bucks.
We all watch as the monster dump-box lifts
and tilts. The blue-black slow-burn payload shifts
then rumbles to the dank, dark space below.
Our radiators, working full-time till
next March, will clank and gurgle, dry the snow
from woolen mittens, intercept the chill
creeping into the house as blizzards blow
pale spoondrift down our street from Beaumont hill.

Skip

The misnamed Grayces own a mutt called Skip,
who chases every bike and car and truck
that makes it down our street. This caper drives
the neighbors nuts. With every yap and yip
we cross our fingers Skip runs out of luck.
But he's been blessed with several hundred lives,
unlike our tomcat, Chance, whose sad demise
under the milk truck took us by surprise.
Old Skip's survived his master's vicious rages,
endured the drunkard's slamming of "the wife",
two daughters' yelps, their flight at tender ages,
but loved the third who bought a hunting knife—
an H.H. Buck—with babysitting wages,
and for some unknown reason took her life.

Thinking of Happiness, She Thinks of That

My Dad brought home a girl's bright red Schwinn bike
we hope will tone his polio-weakened limbs;
but since I'm still too short for it, I sail
on gray slate sidewalk slabs—no two alike—
up by the house of Archie Ray who swims
bare-naked at the Y; then with a Hail
Mary in my heart, take Butler Hill
full-speed-ahead from Dooley's Bar & Grille
and Jake's Garage, a strong wind at my back
pushing me past Merriweather Lane,
my metal wheels repeating clickety-clack,
my roller skate key swinging on its chain,
till, coasting to the Lehigh railroad track,
I catch my breath beside an outbound train.

Robbie Bennett

The Bennetts lived just half a block away.
When Father Flynn came knocking on their door
one sweltering August afternoon, we knew
for sure this wasn't just another day.
Their restless eldest boy had joined the Corps,
his visits back home tense and short and few;
the other one, the timid younger son,
was hiking at the tubs near Laurel Run.
He'd lost his footing on a boulder wet
with algae; others said he took a dare.
None of us will ever quite forget
her feral keen sent ripping through the air,
our monstrous mix of respite and regret
as Father Flynn led all of us in prayer.

Retail Therapy

Joe De Luca was the first to go,
a massive heart attack at thirty-eight.
Next, Tyrone Lake; and though the papers said
it was an accident, we'll never know.
Then stogie-smoking Viktor Novak, freight
conductor for the D&H. All dead
within the space of several months. We paid
our due respects, brought casseroles, and made
novenas for their Holy Souls. We see
the newly-widowed neighbors coffee-klatch,
and by year's end, they're on a shopping spree.
Now Joe's kids' dungarees don't sport a patch,
the Lake and Novak homes are mortgage-free,
and three cleft women's pumps and purses match.

Phil

There's no love lost between the world and Phil,
the creepy kid who lives six houses down,
who brags about the time he swung a cat
and let it fly; the noose up on Tank Hill
for puppy dogs that might refuse to drown;
the day he skinned alive a sewer rat.
So when they're picking sides for sandlot ball,
Phil is the name the boys will never call.
I watch him wait for someone to relent,
lend him a bat, toss him the catcher's mitt
or even send him to right field. He'll vent—
for now at least—with epithets and spit,
or maybe shoot the bird, impenitent,
slouching home to sins he must commit.

Bully

Eddie Fox is sly beyond his years,
his unsuspecting parents' pride and joy.
A rascal always spoiling for a fight,
Eddie boasts there's not a soul he fears.
The hit-and-run is Eddie's favorite ploy;
his alibis are always watertight.
The other boys won't flip their baseball cards
with Eddie. Moms won't let him in their yards.
Last week the object of his spite became
a little girl he thought would hardly pose
a threat; but Kitty Kramer foiled his game,
gave him a shiner and a bloody nose.
Now Eddie Fox seems chastened, tempered, tame;
or is he seething? Heaven only knows.

Grouper

In a stately home next-door to Mr. Cooper,
the Donovans hole up behind white oaks,
a high box hedge and windows louver-shuttered.
They had a son the bully boys tagged "Grouper",
the butt of snickering and nasty jokes,
who cracked his knuckles, bit his lips, and stuttered.
An altar boy and would-be Eagle Scout,
he had a thing for knots. He seemed devout.
Though at the time too young to comprehend
the incidental whisper of a word
by busybody neighbors, in the end
we disentangled what we'd overheard.
His note thanked Kitty—Grouper's only friend—
to whom he left his taws and Mynah bird.

Nanny Brown

The Grayces' next-door neighbor, Hannah Brown,
whom everyone calls "Nanny Brown," lives with
her aged, ailing father. Never wed,
old Nanny trudges every day to town
to waitress at the Woolworth's counter. Myth
has it she ties "Daddy" to his bed
so he won't wander off while she's away.
This may be true. Last year, on Christmas Day,
we tracked his errant footprints in the snow
from Nanny's sidewalk, past O'Hara's bar,
then up the hill to Sacred Heart. Although
we found him, for he hadn't gotten far,
they had to amputate the baby toe
it's rumored Nanny's pickled in a jar.

Realpolitik

Autumn 1960. First foray
into the world of party politics.
As neighbors hang their posters up, I flinch—
amid the sea of signs for JFK
ours is the only house displaying Dick's
bushy brows and slogan. *He's a cinch
to win, a shoo-in*, father firmly states,
claiming Nixon's won all four debates.
For weeks, I am an outcast at my school
where Sister Agnes has us pray so that
Jack Kennedy will win. The ridicule
redoubles once the charming Democrat
becomes our 35th. My mom, no fool,
in February buys a pillbox hat.

Intermezzo

Preserve your memories, a song suggests,
they're all that's left you. Whether foul or fair,
they point to who we were, who we've become.
We've entertained a few November guests;
our bangled, tangled, raggy, shaggy hair
has turned the whitest shade of pale, and some
of our best friends have died or moved away.
In looking back on our naïveté,
I can't recall, in this meandering,
if Chet and David mentioned Emmett Till
or Rosa Parks or Martin Luther King;
for troubles at our patch town flour mill
and breakers overshadowed everything
from Philly all the way to Jacksonville.

"Doc" Baumann

No architects or bankers grace our block;
just tradesmen, office clerks, a nurse or two,
a teacher, mailman, meter maid, mechanic,
scores of housewives. Not a single doc.
That is, unless you count the Baumann crew
Fred Kramer called this morning in a panic
because a lightning bolt crevassed our tree,
crushing his brand-new Buick Century.
Tree Surgeon says the sign on Baumann's door;
so, armed with chainsaws, ladders, wedges, ropes,
Doc and the guys excise the sycamore
without the need for clamps or stethoscopes.
One hundred forty rings run round its core—
that's thirty presidents, eleven popes.

Cat Lady

Mildred Smith has recently retired
from Ladies' Lingerie at Pomeroy's.
Her cats, all orphaned strays, now benefit
from Mildred's full-time care. She has acquired
a good half-dozen, say the Harris boys,
the twins who live next-door. Her favorite
is Tina, who escaped from Phil last year
with one blind eye and only half an ear.
Mildred would have made a loving wife
and mother, but it's too late. Anyhow,
she seems to be contented with her life;
for though the Harris twins mewl out *Meow!*
Meow! when Mildred passes by, the knife
of their derision cannot wound her now.

Changing of the Guard

The elderly McBrides were quiet folk
whose claim to fame was that, on Halloween,
they'd hand us kids a nickel if we made
them laugh. A silly song, a corny joke
was all it took. He was an ex-Marine,
wore medals to the Veterans Day parade;
she was the quintessential Southern belle,
who'd die before she'd utter *damn* or *hell*.
Overnight, it seems to me, they're gone,
supplanted by the Dukes, a family
of eight. Now trash cans line the unkempt lawn,
and Mr. Duke, who sports a trim goatee,
will often disappear from dusk till dawn,
while she can be heard swearing. Royally.

Strange Gods

Just one street west, on Main, Episcopalians
will socialize next Sunday on the broad
expanse outside their hall, weather permitting.
I'm leery of them. Not that they are aliens,
but we've been taught there's only One True God.
Ours. My going there would mean committing
heresy, were I to dare partake
of their whipped cream, their strawberries, their cake.
And so I wait. But wait. Come mid-July's
annual shindig, blessed with Catholic prayer,
boxty, cabbage rolls and pasty pies,
all stripes of Protestants have come to share
our festival. Next June I'll do likewise,
though I be damned. Though mother yank my hair.

Kidnapped

One summer, after dark, when all the bats
had come and gone, and we'd squeezed diamond rings
from lightning bugs we'd captured in a jar,
we heard the screeches (Was it Mildred's cats,
we wondered, or the Dukes, those ding-a-lings
across the street); when all at once a car
with Alabama plates, a blue Bel-Air,
rushed by, then later, staties everywhere.
Marie Bell's brutal ex had forced his way
into her house and snatched young Jimmy, who
had just been put to bed. Somewhere, someday
the cops might get a tip and follow through;
that is, if Jimmy's in the USA,
not gone, as some folks fear, to Timbuktu.

Mrs. Moffat

She's out there early with her rubber gloves
and Comet cleanser, scowling at the smudge
or speck she may have overlooked last time.
I wonder whether Mrs. Moffat loves
the dull endeavors of the household drudge
or simply hates the mere idea of grime.
The mailman and the paperboy are wary
of Mrs. Moffat. Children think she's scary.
She scours her front porch steps and even sweeps
the little swath of dirt that runs between
the sidewalk and the curb; and though she keeps
her panes impeccable, her storm door clean,
who's to know if Mrs. Moffat weeps
when no one rings her bell on Halloween.

Ragman

April, and the ragman's come around
with fingerless gloves, and a greasy leather pouch
jingling with the pennies he will pay
for other people's junk, three cents a pound.
Grizzled, grimy, something of a grouch,
he speaks like someone come from far away.
He'll buy old pipes and pulleys, bottles, scraps
of cloth and metal, magazines, perhaps
a little holy terror now and then
(according to our moms and dads); and so
it's no surprise to all the neighbors, when
we hear the ragman's tiny tin horn blow
announcing he's come down our street again,
that Phil and Eddie opt to lie real low.

Mea culpa

Ringing his bell, old Ciccio Antony,
the ice cream man, arrives. For just five cents
you get to taste the flavor-of-the-day,
but on your birthday, two big dips for free.
Having had enough of indigence
that sweltering Fourth, and knowing I might pay
a hefty price, I coolly jumped the line,
barefacedly alleged I'd just turned nine,
then claimed my purple prize. But someone knew
I'd come into the world in January.
Wasting not a minute, Eddie blew
the whistle on my luscious boysenberry
sin. Still, I got off with just a few
Our Fathers and a fervent Hail Mary.

Boots

When Mr. Cooper died at ninety-three
his house was rented out in no time flat;
for who would buy a rundown clapboard painted
what kindly Mrs. Lake called "burgundy"?
Still, the gentle man who'd tipped his hat
was missed; so Mrs. Moffat nearly fainted
when in moved Boots, her mother and her daughter
(Tsk-tsk, born out of wedlock!); but I thought her
cool. They called her Boots because she wore
red high-heeled boots no matter where she went.
Phil's father claimed she was a two-bit whore
who had to turn cheap tricks to pay the rent.
But after Boots decamped to Baltimore,
I'd ape her swagger to my heart's content.

Fire

The frequent sorrows in our neighborhood—
the youngest Grayce girl and the Bennett boy,
three Lambert infants dying one by one
of CF (something not yet understood)—
eclipse our piddling stretches of pure joy
and betterment, hardscrabble and hard-won.
The night the Dorsey family died, my trust
in God's all-wise, all-merciful, all-just
core attributes was tested. No one knew
what caused the blaze; some said it had to be
faulty wiring, a blocked-up chimney flue,
or lights on their aluminum Christmas tree.
A vacant lot now stands as witness to
the distance of some loving deity.

Kitty Kramer

There's Kitty Kramer, racing double-quick
on that red Schwinn of hers, a baseball card
clacking in the spokes. She lives next-door
in an ancient double-block of ghetto brick
with thirteen double cousins whose back yard
is way too tame for Kitty anymore.
You won't catch Kitty on the hopscotch squares
or jumping rope. She's game for double dares.
Last spring it was those roller skates, and soon
she'll drive her Daddy's big black Pontiac.
As Kitty flies this summer afternoon,
I see a girl who jams the luggage rack,
indifferent to the way the Full Crow Moon
trails a bus that won't be doubling back.

Coda

So here we are, approaching three score ten,
"Boomers" from a lost millennium,
perched on Simon's metaphoric park
bench, waiting, musing, *I remember when* . . .,
wise to what we knew, and what has come
to light since days of dancing in the dark.
And if we misremember, fantasize,
omitting secrets, cover-ups and lies—
the boys flown to the belly of the beast,
the pennyroyal cure, the preemie fraud,
the tender mercies of the parish priest—
cut us some slack. Our innocence was flawed:
we failed to spot the specter at the feast,
and every one of us believed in God.

IV.

Other Folk

Far into the Lives of Other Folk

I knew a tale of a better kind.
—Robert Frost, "On the Heart's Beginning to Cloud the Mind"

You could be anyone or anywhere—
the checkout lady at the A&P,
the glib *poseur* with attitude and hair,
the full-sleeve-tattooed ER orderly,
the Walmart shelver on the graveyard shift,
the goody-two-shoes or the evil twin,
the badass mom, the waitress who's been stiffed,
the sergeant notifying next of kin.

No matter who you are, I presuppose
a motivation, blessing or regret,
inventing possible scenarios,
each storyline a fanciful vignette,
symmetrical and always well-defined:
bold, italicized and underlined.

Of course, this works both ways. It's only fair
to wonder what you must concoct for me
as you observe the blatant wear and tear
that time has left for all the world to see.
I claim your offhand gift of shortest shrift—
it's tough to see beyond the crepe-like skin,
the balding crown, the thoughts that tend to drift,
the turkey wattle underneath the chin.

You see me eye the piercings in your nose
and tongue at Betty's Coin-Op Launderette;
but as we sit and watch our spinning clothes,
we joke about a lost sock and forget
cross-purposes, then ultimately find
we've let the heart begin to cloud the mind.

Roxham Road

For the families crossing through the woods into Canada

A New York Trailways bus has pulled into
its final U.S. stop: the Mountain Mart
Mobil Station, Plattsburgh, passing through
to Montreal, scheduled to depart
at 1 a.m. A family alights.
Retrieving their baggage from the cargo hold,
they huddle with their backs against the night's
brutal wind and Adirondack cold.

I drive them in my cab up to Champlain,
to Roxham Road's dead-end, where there's a trench
to navigate, a trek through rough terrain,
formalities in English and in French.
I light their way and wait until they've crossed.
At last it clicks. That dire word. Tempest-tost.

—*Saint-Bernard-de-Lacolle, Québec, February 2017*

Shakespeare's Sisters

i. Suzy

> *Draw near and bestow grace upon my song.*
> —*Homeric Hymn XXIV*, to Hestia

A woman in her seventh decade peels
potatoes at the kitchen sink. Nearby,
the washer slogs a load of clothes. A pie
dough's setting in the fridge. Her home-cooked meals
and fresh-pressed linens speak of household bliss
—as do the spotless windows, bath and floor—
at length, like an extended metaphor.
She tends her garden. Nothing is amiss.

But there are scribblings in a cookie tin.
She hesitates, then feeds them to the fire
as if engaging in a sacred duty.
Once they have burned, she flours the rolling pin,
singing to herself of vain desire
and all he'll never hear of truth and beauty.

ii. "Poetisa"

i.m. María Eugenia Vaz Ferreira, Uruguayan poet

Morning is due to all—
To some—the Night—
—Emily Dickinson, from Poem #1577

The mild pampero wafts a balm of pine
and eucalyptus through the spindrift air.
She draws the velvet curtains as each sign
of life appears: shadow-fish clouds tear
the sky apart; a lone hornero peeps;
a benteveo calls. Then all too soon—
though now it seems to her the whole world sleeps
unmindful of a waning austral moon—
the customary rough, pragmatic clamor
of trams and city workmen will dispel
beatitude with bugle-honk and hammer;
while, lifting like a vampire pipistrelle,
a daring line takes off for distant caves
as she pours coffee. Butters toast. Behaves.

iii. Cinéma Vérité

Is there no play to ease the anguish of a torturing hour?
—William Shakespeare, *A Midsummer Night's Dream*

Her carpet isn't red. Gram's old rag rugs
jazz up the floor. No Stuart Weitzman heels
or loan-out emeralds from Tiffany's.
She's slender, sober, isn't into drugs
—except for all those Sominex pastilles—
yet hasn't made the list of nominees.

So she auditions for *The Perfect Wife*
and snags the leading role. This slice-of-life
feature film, shot in a single take
in Hi-Def format, ultimately draws
an audience of one. She fails to fake
indifference to Oscar-night applause
because she's gone through hell for heaven's sake,
and time is running out for last hurrahs.

Multiverse

i.m. Beth Davidson Shotton

And though she feels as if she's in a play, she is anyway.
    —The Beatles, *Penny Lane*

The pretty nurse in Penny Lane is dead.
She played her part until the curtain fell.
Or is her troupe booked somewhere else instead?

Although those notes are earworms in my head—
the trumpet solo and the engine bell—
the pretty nurse in Penny Lane is dead.

The barber and the banker long since fled
the roundabout. The fireman as well.
Can they be working somewhere else instead?

The neighborhood's a tourist trap, it's said;
no poppies like the ones she used to sell.
The pretty nurse in Penny Lane is dead.

Or is she? Maybe we have been misled,
and other Penny Lanes spin, parallel,
in quantum time, to other tunes instead.

I'm clinging to one final, chronon shred
of hope. As far as anyone can tell,
the pretty nurse in Penny Lane is dead,
and may be living somewhere else instead.

Hapax legomenon

> According to S.P. Rosenbaum's *A Concordance to
> the Poems of Emily Dickinson*, the word "fish" occurs
> only once in her poems (#1749).

I wonder if Emily was channeling
Achilles' taunt to Lykaon,
heaved into the deep and swirling
waters of the River Xanthos;

or maybe second mate Stubb,
declaiming, on the deck of the *Pequod*,
through astral signs and wonders
his final resting place,

when, in her tale of death,
the voyager is hastened—
mute and objectified—
by a whispering billow

to an appalling heaven
of shriven glass and fish.

Nines

The metric system did not really catch on in the States, unless you count the increasing popularity of the nine-millimeter bullet.
—Dave Barry

When I was in first grade
—*Catherine*—
we had regular fire drills, just like now,
orderly evacuations onto the schoolyard,
usually on a fine fall or spring day.
The teachers did a roll call
as we shuffled back to class
—*Allison, Avielle, Caroline, Charlotte, Chase,
Dylan, Emilie, Jack, Jessica, Josephine, Kyle, Olivia*—

Later, when I was a little older
—*Cassie, Corey*—
there were duck-and-cover civil defense drills.
We'd practice hiding under our desks
—*Kelly, Kyle*—
in case of a nuclear fireball from an atomic bomb.
Maybe your grandparents
told you stories about those times
—*Lauren, Lena, Steven*—

Now they have lockdown drills
—*Ana, Anna, Daniel, Daniel, Daniel*—
color-codes, metal detectors
—*Madeleine, Marian, Mary, Matthew, James, John*—
designated hiding-places
closets, corners
where active shooters
can never, ever, find you
—*Noah, Rachel, Benjamin, Jesse, Naomi, Isaiah,*

Grace—

Χάος

Chaos speaks a language of its own—
a lexicon of howl, hue and cry;
a dialect that contradicts the lie
of rationality. Its bone-on-bone
inflection duplicates the wordless moan,
and parses the wild syllable of why.
It deconstructs all goodness from good-bye
with syllabaries rigorous as stone.

The idiom of Chaos can translate
with ease the accent of a South Atlantic
gale, the timbre of a red-tailed hawk
before the kill. It will not mitigate—
sprung from the pen's sweet ordered lines—the frantic,
bounding pulse. Declining double-talk

and claptrap, Chaos gives it to us straight.

Family at Sunset Beach, California

She digs to China, as her parents sit
on beach chairs, staring out to sea. The line
of the horizon beckons, counterfeit.
The young girl's faith is pure and genuine.
I recognize the commonplace tableau,
and know that, though they sport a winsome guise,
there are some places Mom and Dad won't go
despite their cache of infinite Julys.

For as they lounge there, temperate and tanned,
the water rises, flustering the child;
so they will shepherd her to Disneyland
where she will be enchanted and beguiled,
while stars outnumber every grain of sand
and zero sums remain unreconciled.

shadow art streaming from sly stone angels

i.

the mute roar
billows still
in one singing
shadow
marked faintly
like dubious
reason

ii.

art created eternity
and the mystery
all this unfurled
between
beneath
and O
on

iii.

late shy lovers
fields of perfumed
lights
songs from streams
perfect and
now
forgotten

iv.

between a love and
bridges
stone vaults
I kneel inert
nothing
free
could I?

v.

not with
the tulip's death
these angels
of faith
cannot touch
your unimaginable
air

vi.

the day remaining
sly survivor
living danger
foolish
fruit half-green
hard dying
in love

vii.

dispossessed
nothing
the caught world
magnificent and blue
tiny streaming
living sacrament
no room

For Tim, on the Eve of Battle

For Tim Murphy

This charge I commit unto thee, son Timothy, according to the prophecies which went before on thee, that thou by them mightest war a good warfare.
—1 Timothy 1:18

The rattles, caws and clicks of circling crows
outdo the western meadowlark of late;
flickertails in burrows hibernate
in colonies till spring; and I suppose
your fields are carpeted with winter's snows,
your hunting boots and Winnie 28
cleaned and set aside. They'll have to wait,
like Chucky who looks up at you, and knows.

Yet soon the great Red River, frozen now,
will recommence its northward course, and pink
wild prairie roses bloom beneath the fair
cerulean High Plains skies. Farmers will plow
their acres once again.   Let not your ink
run dry, my friend. Fear not the trumpet's blare.

—January 2018

Votive

Saint Joseph's Oratory, Montreal.
Between the crypt and dark magmatic rock
of the mountain's flank, along a blue-domed hall
one hundred four feet long, I slowly walk.
Ex-votos hanging on the chapel wall—
canes and crutches—testify *en bloc*
to gratitude and grace. This same motif
repeats in eight imposing bas-reliefs.

Although I've come here many times to pray
for family and friends, to make a deal
with God—through blessèd, sainted, Frère André
Bessette—to write intentions down, to kneel
and kiss the relic, I am here today,
amid ten thousand candles, this surreal
disorienting ambience of grief
and hope, to test my limits of belief:

a candle for each of the twenty-six
gunned down at Sandy Hook. Each nascent flame,
fragile yet deadly, flickers on the wicks,
irresolute as doubt, yet hot as shame.
So as I watch the self-sustaining mix
burn down, I mourn, yet curse the waiting game
in Washington, the sad misguided thief
of time, the dates unbearable and brief.

Edward Hopper Triptych

Early Sunday Morning (1930)

> *In every work of genius we recognize our own rejected thoughts; they come back to us with a certain alienated majesty.*
> —Ralph Waldo Emerson (from *Self-Reliance*)

There's something comforting and intimate
        about the line of small shops in the glare
        of Sunday morning. Something clean and spare,
        bounded but suggesting infinite
extent. Then all at once we take a hit
        to the solar plexus—we become aware
        of storefront windows whispering *Beware,*
        and that the quietude is counterfeit.
The atmosphere is placidly bereft,
        devoid of movement and of human face;
        the softened desolation of the street
suggests a hyper-emptiness, a trace
        of absent presences, a bittersweet
        tristesse, as though the world has just been left
                alone to face the heft
of enigmatic darkness to the right,
a monolith that leads our line of sight—
                through Hopper's scumbled light—
away from consolation toward concern
as we approach our point of no return.

Pentimento: *High Noon* (1949)

There is a sort of elation about sunlight on the upper part of a house.
—Edward Hopper

The plain white clapboard house is hanging fire—
half-drawn shades, an inching of the space
between the curtain lace, the artifice
high on the kitchen wall. The yawning door.

She stares, in high-heeled shoes and loose peignoir,
at someone or some thing beyond the grass
that leads, it seems, to nowhere. At a loss,
she's free to leave, and yet a prisoner.

Will she renounce the solitude of sky,
the stark elation of this prairie noon,
the beauty of her world, Euclidean,
blinding in its pure geometry,
to trust, for once, a sudden aperçu,
and flee those two extremes of cinnamon?

Pennsylvania Coal Town (1947)

The patch town isn't specified. It could
be one of many, like the nondescript
dwellings—all identical—of wood,
their little plots well-tended, borders clipped.
I spot a hobnail milk glass table lamp,
lace curtains, pictures on the parlor wall.
This relic of a former mining camp
is mapped far from my house in Montreal.
Sunlight strikes a terra cotta urn
from which there sprouts a weather-beaten fern.

A man—the owner? renter?—takes a break
and looks at something far beyond my gaze.
The shadowed cart, the stationary rake
are faintly reminiscent of Millet's
L'Angélus. But this man doesn't bow
his head in prayer. He's simply tired and hot.
Perhaps he'll take a rag and wipe his brow,
resume his work without a second thought.
Or maybe, having had enough, undone,
he'll curse the clapboard baking in the sun.

Fast forward fifty years. The man is dead.
Black diamonds blasted from the Northern Field
of ridge-and-valley Appalachia fed
our furnaces. All adits have been sealed.
Abandoned breakers loom above the town
that's been declared the fourth worst place to live
in Pennsylvania. Life is tumbledown.
But this I know is true: that I would give
my eyeteeth for the chance to tell the man
in Hopper's painting, *Love it while you can.*

V.

The Watchers

The Watchers at Punta Ballena, Uruguay

They come in droves. As afternoon subsides
they settle on this bluff above the shore.
La Plata's mixed semidiurnal tides
cannot provide an explanation for
this pilgrimage; nor can the jasmine- and
the eucalyptus-scented air. Baleen
whales passed this spot some months ago. At hand,
the expectation of a flash of green.

But maybe they are here, like me, to trace
the shimmering horizon of the sea,
to scan it for a master plan, for grace
beyond its incandescence, where they see
some human promise in the sun's decline—
a deep though distant sense of the divine.

Su casa es mi casa

Secret Swig

To the frail and the fragile,
the fugitive and the shallow;
to the irrational,
the illogical and the immoral;
to all that is frivolous,
flimsy, fickle and finite;
to smoke rings,
thyrsus roses,
waves of sea foam,
and the mists of oblivion . . .
to the little bindles
poor pilgrims carry
as they wander through this cruel, crazy
transient world, I raise a toast
with fleeting words
and heady wines
sparkling with bubbles
in brittle glasses . . .

—María Eugenia Vaz Ferreira (1875-1924), "Vaso furtivo" (*La isla de los cánticos,* 1924)

The Split

It was a chain as strong as Fate,
sacred as a life, sensitive as a soul;
I broke it with a lily and continue on my journey
with Death's magnificent indifference . . . with calm

curiosity my spirit peers out of its inner pool
and the mirror of sleeping waters
reflects a god or a monster, masked as a
dark sphinx bewildered by other lives.

—Delmira Agustini (1886-1914), "La ruptura" (*Los cálices vacíos,* 1913)

Daybreak

This is the hour when the ashen dawn, newly broken free from night, turns translucent, fresh, barefoot, and joyful, and morning falls upon the black earth. The light of Venus pales amid the wondrous wild hymn of living things. In this hour of intoxicating rapture, I forget the past and the future, evil and goodness, the tears I have wept and those I surely have yet to weep. I forget that my son is of mortal flesh who one day must die; and leaning against a damp fencepost I begin to sing. I sing, sing, sing, with a clear voice and an uncluttered heart, as if now, this morning, I and the worn-out world were absolutely new and pure.

—Juana de Ibarbourou (1892-1979), "El alba" (*El cántaro fresco*, 1920)

Midday

Transparent the air, transparent
the sickle of morning,
the warm white hills, the gestures of waves,
it is all sea, all that sea carrying out
its deep task,
the sea lost in thought,
the sea, at that honeyed hour when instinct
hums like a drowsy bee . . .
Sun, love, open lilies, seascapes,
golden limbs sensitive and tender as bodies,
the vast pale sands.

Transparent the air, transparent
the voices, the silence.
On the edge of love, of the sea, of the morning,
on the hot sand, trembling in its whiteness,
each one is a fruit ripening into death.

—Idea Vilariño (1920-2009), "Mediodía" from "Verano"
(*La suplicante,* 1944)

Housework

I shake off cobwebs from the dismantled
sky
with the same duster
I use every day,
I shake off the lowly dust
from the same old things, I dust,
I dust the stardust, always the same
cosmic demolition, the forever-dead caress
that blankets earthly furniture,
I clean doors and windows, I clean
their glass in order to see more clearly,
I sweep the floor covered with garbage,
shriveled leaves, ashes,
crumbs, footprints,
glittering bones,
I sweep the soil, deeper, the soil,
and I'm making a deep hole
as the need arises.

—Amanda Berenguer (1921-2010), "Tarea doméstica"
(*Quehaceres e invenciones*, 1963)

Residual

Long life, short life,
everything in our lives is reduced
to a grey residue in memory.

All that is left of former travels
are enigmatic coins
with counterfeit claims.

All that remains of memory
is some dust and a certain fragrance.
Can this, by chance, be poetry?

—Ida Vitale (1923-), "Residua" (*Parvo reino,* 1984)

Poem X

This melon is a rose.
It smells like a rose.
There must be an angel inside it
with a passionate, blazing heart.
It is a saint;
everything it touches
turns to gold and perfume;
it has every virtue, it is flawless.
I pray to it,
and later I am going to write a poem about it.
Now, I only state what it is:
a bolt of lightning,
a perfume,
the son of roses.

—Marosa di Giorgio (1932-2004), "Poema X" (*Magnolia*, 1965)

Steps

Small, persistent changes.

Beneath the sky there is already a degree
of brilliance or of coolness.

More dust has settled on the floor or on the chair.

A tiny wrinkle appears or deepens.

There is a new nuance in the sound
of a familiar voice (Would you notice it?)

Amid the muddled chorus of mixed voices
some are missing, others
appear.

The same
sum total: nothing has changed.

The millionth wave strikes
the millionth rock
and the erosion
subtle and sure
continues.

—Circe Maia (1932-), "Escalones" (*Cambios, permanencias,* 1978)

Prayer

Deliver us, Lord,
from meeting up,
years later,
with the loves of our lives.

—Cristina Peri Rossi (1941-), "Oración" (*Inmovilidad de los barcos*, 1997)

Broken Poem

I'm taking pages from the river
and when I say river
I mean the sound of birds perching together on their usual
branches
only to break away into the melted sky
No. I yank pages from the river
That is to say—I'm trying to do the impossible
You can't hold back the river
You can't take every single page from the river
in order to stop what is written in its waters
But I'm taking pages from the river
This is how I define myself. And I'm doing it
I cross a shadow. But the river is a happy machine.
It exists apart from me. It doesn't wait for me, nor does it change
and I write alone
I wouldn't call myself "drowned", but I think the river
writes versions that I dilute later on
feeling my problem focusing
Anyway, the pages write themselves
and I'm alone when I write
and try to take pages from the river

—Paula Einöder (1974-), "Poema roto" (*Árbol experimental,* 2004)

La Niña

Above our field of stunted corn and thistle,
a lone chimango circles, scouts, homes in
as sure and swift and savage as a missile,
pins down a leveret, rips away its skin,
ignores the terror-stricken eyes, the squeal,
devours the pulsing heart. His thirst now slaked,
he leaves the rest for a carancho's meal.

The land is quivering, crumbling, cracked and caked,
the stream a silent checkerboard of mud,
the well near dry. This scarcity of water
will either have me own the guts, the blood,
the rational, inexorable slaughter;
or, as I turn my eyes to Crux, renew
my faith in tussocks starred with morning dew.

—Saladillo, Argentina, January 2009

Dawn

day breaks on the silver sea
the bay still in shadows
daybreak of white jasmine and blue hortensia
scent of eucalyptus

there are no sea lions in the bay
only fishing boats slipping away through shadows
past the tip of the peninsula
out to the silver sea

the bay is ringed with boulders
the sand is still cool
sea lions lift their heads
on their island in the silver sea

a giant hand rises from Playa Brava
it warns and beckons
the wind and shadows catch warnings
the giant hand has let slip away

there are no swimmers
in the silver sea at daybreak
only cormorants perched on the boulders
their black wings shimmering in the sun

daybreak of wind and water
a statue amid rocks and mussel shells
a blue and white statue of *Stella Maris*
her back to the shimmering silver sea

Ending

Nothing to reproach or to forgive.
Nothing to unwind or to unweave.
No arguments to prove or to disprove.
No wrongs to right. No rights to claim or waive.
In retrospect, it's all so relative—
seasons, space-time, truth and make-believe.
I've left the northern hemisphere, but you've
a motto: *Plus ça change* . . . I hear you;
                                                save
that here the jasmine is in bloom. Above,
Crux reappears to complement a mauve
and apricot tableau. The men arrive,
back from the long November cattle drive,
while in a nearby eucalyptus grove
a golden-eared paloma coos his love.

Celebration

A wash of molten silver slips along
the rippled black of Maldonado Bay
beneath this month's blue moon. A well-heeled throng
spills from the restos, as she weaves her way
among them with a folding canvas chair
down to the docks, far from all the fuss.
No grapes to scarf, no new red underwear,
la gringa feels de trop, superfluous.

As rockets blaze, the revelers *ooh* and *ah;*
then when the party's over, rev their cars,
burn rubber round the dark peninsula
till daybreak clears the sky of lingering stars;
while she remains and welcomes in the year
watching as petrels dive then reappear.

—Punta del Este, Uruguay, December 31, 2009

Scintillae

Sky of verdigris. Ocean of slate.
Threadbare clouds shapeshift,
scatter, then disintegrate,
their essence gone
the way of plans which, once discarded, drift

from consciousness. She puts the coffee on,
lights a cigarette,
attends the morning dénouement,
the daily snare
of memories that give rise to regret

for what was real: a creaky seventh stair,
an ivy-patterned wall,
a simple oaken Morris chair,
a ceiling crack,
a chifforobe behemoth in a hall,

a red Formica table, bric-a-brac,
umbrellas by a door,
a girl who once would sit and track
beveled beams
inching their way across a kitchen floor . . .

but not this one. An overspill of dreams
has come once more to whelm,
inexorably, as streams
are drawn into
the sea. And from that pure and loving realm,

her fountain pen with ink of peacock blue.

Watershed

Here are your waters and your watering place.
Drink and be whole again beyond confusion.
—Robert Frost, "Directive"

I rode the rapids of the Iguazú
and flew above the falls at Devil's Throat.
I sailed the Beagle Channel on a boat
that nearly capsized as it ran into
an unexpected squall. I skirted by
the bergs on Lago Argentino, crossed
the Jaguarão, the Plate, and nearly lost
my bearings in Brazil and Uruguay.

Those were the waters of the wild in me.
Now time has tamed the tenor of my dream
and I am drawn back to the source, the stream
I disregarded as an absentee—
the Susquehanna, ancient, faithful, strong.
The river that had borne me, all along.

VI.

Pointing Home

Pointing Home

All things on earth point home in old October:
sailors to sea, travelers to walls and fences,
hunters to field and hollow and the long voice
of the hounds, the lover to the love he has forsaken.
   —Thomas Wolfe, *Of Time and the River*

In expectation of approaching winter,
a woodchuck slips into his grass-lined burrow;
the fall migration of the vesper sparrow
begins, as afternoons grow shorter, fainter.

The blood moon of the Abenaki hunter
wanes, as mercury glissades toward zero:
apprentice to the North, I'll need to borrow
the mettle of a born and bred Vermonter.

And so, when mountain winds conspire to wither
asters, mums and marigolds; as mice
prepare their cellar nests; before snow flurries
sweep against the windowpanes, I gather
pitch-pine kindling for the fireplace,
and from the riverbank, late elderberries.

Notes

We. This poem is a sonnenizio, a form invented by poet Kim Addonizio. The first line is from Timothy Murphy's Nemerov Award-winning sonnet, "The Track of the Storm." The word "we" appears in every line, mainly within other words.

Far into the Lives of Other Folk. Robert Frost once told a group of students, *I never know where I'll write or what I'll write. I remember once in Wilkes-Barre, Pennsylvania, stuck there, changing trains, so I had to go to a hotel, and I wrote one of my best poems right there in that hotel, standing on my head. A curious state comes over you, that's all.—Robert Frost: A Lover's Quarrel with the World, Part 1,* minute 18. The poem he was referring to is "On the Heart's Beginning to Cloud the Mind."

Shakespeare's Sisters. The poem's title was inspired by Chapter 3 of Virginia Woolf's *A Room of One's Own*. Note on "Suzy": The name "Suzy" refers to "Suzy Homemaker." Note on "Poetisa": The antiquated word *poetisa* meaning *poetess,* has now been replaced by the word *poeta,* meaning poet, male or female. The hornero and the benteveo are birds common to Uruguay. From the mid-19th to the early 20th century, a horseman with a bugle rode ahead of the trams in Montevideo as a warning to pedestrians.

Multiverse. George F. R. Ellis, philosopher and cosmologist, remains skeptical of the existence of the multiverse. Nevertheless, he writes: *Parallel universes may or may not exist; the case is unproved. We are going to have to live with that uncertainty.—* from "Does the Multiverse Really Exist?", *Scientific American* (August 2011). Beth Davidson was a childhood friend of John Lennon and the inspiration for the line about the pretty nurse in the song *Penny Lane*. Beth Davidson went on to marry John's best friend, Pete Shotton, and she remained a member of the Beatles' close circle of friends until her death from cancer at the age of thirty-five.

Nines. The names in this poem are the given names of the thirty-seven children murdered at Columbine High School, West Nickel Mines School, and Sandy Hook Elementary School by hostile intruders armed with 9 mm weapons. Nine millimeters is equal to slightly less than three-eighths of an inch. This poem was written before the Stoneman Douglas High School shooting.

shadow art streaming from sly stone angels. This poem is a series of erasure/compression sonnets taken from the following sonnets by women poets whose lifetimes span the past two hundred years: "Written Near a Port on a Dark Evening" by Charlotte Smith (1749-1806), "To a Daisy" by Alice Christina Meynell (1847-1922), "Sonnet" by Alice Dunbar-Nelson (1875-1935), "Praise" by Jane Cooper (1924-2007), "Aperture" by Ann Lauterbach (1942-), "Foolishly, Halved, I See You" by Elizabeth Macklin (1952-) and "Sonnet in E" by April Bernard (1956-).

Secret Swig. A clue to the meaning of the term *thyrsus roses* may be found in poem 32 of Charles Baudelaire's *Le spleen de Paris*, where the thyrsus, in its essential duality, represents the power of the irrational as well as the rational with respect to creativity. Baudelaire's reference to the feminine aspect of the symbolic thyrsus is also of significance in this poem by Vaz Ferreira.

Midday. Ana Inés Larre Borges, literary executor for Idea Vilariño, granted permission for me to translate "Mediodía" on condition that I include the original Spanish version as an end note. *Mediodía/Transparentes los aires, transparentes/ la hoz de la mañana,/los blancos montes tibios, los gestos de las olas,/ todo ese mar, todo ese mar que cumple/ su profunda tarea,/el mar ensimismado,/ el mar, a esa hora de miel en que el instinto/zumba como una abeja/somnolienta.../Sol, amor, azucenas dilatadas, marinas,/ Ramas rubias sensibles y tiernas como cuerpos,/ vastas arenas pálidas./ Transparentes los aires, transparentes/ las voces, el silencio./ A orillas del amor, del mar, de la mañana,/ en la arena caliente, temblante de blancura,/ cada uno es un fruto madurando su muerte./* (from the poem "Verano", *Poesía Completa,* Editorial Cal y Canto, Mayo 2010).

La Niña. The Argentine drought of 2008-2009 was partly caused by the natural phenomenon known as La Niña, resulting in catastrophic losses of livestock and crops. The word niña also means girl. The chimango and the carancho are two birds of prey common to the Argentine pampas. Crux is the Southern Cross constellation, visible only in the Southern hemisphere.

Celebration. It is a New Year's Eve custom in Spain and in many Latin American countries to eat a green grape on each stroke of midnight, and to wear a new red undergarment, for good luck during the coming year.

About the Author

Catherine Chandler, an American-born poet, is the author of *The Frangible Hour*, winner of the 2016 Richard Wilbur Award (University of Evansville Press); *Lines of Flight* (Able Muse Press), shortlisted for the Poets' Prize, *Glad and Sorry Seasons* (Biblioasis), and *This Sweet Order* (White Violet Press), as well as two chapbooks, *For No Good Reason* and *All or Nothing*. Her complete bio, podcasts, reviews, a list of awards and other information are available online at cathychandler.blogspot.com. Catherine currently lives in Saint-Lazare-de-Vaudreuil, Québec and Punta del Este, Uruguay.

Made in the USA
Monee, IL
15 July 2021